BLACK-NECKED STILT (CHICK)
Himantopus mexicanus

MIGRATING DUCKS, GEESE, AND SWANS
Mt. Shasta from Tule Lake, Tule Lake National Wildlife Refuge, Siskiyou County

GREAT EGRET *Ardea alba*
Martinez Regional Shoreline, Contra Costa County

CALIFORNIA GULL *Larus californicus*
Mono Basin Scenic Area, Mono County

Opposite: FORSTER'S TERN *Sterna forsteri*
Bolsa Chica Ecological Reserve, Orange County

Wild Birds
OF CALIFORNIA

RUSS KERR

DAVID LUKAS

COMPANION PRESS
SANTA BARBARA, CALIFORNIA

MORGAN BALL

MARBLED GODWITS *Limosa fedoa*

Companion Press
464 Terrace Road
Santa Barbara, California 93109

Jane Freeburg, Publisher
Mark Schlenz, Editor
Designed by Lucy Brown
Printed and bound in Hong Kong
through Bolton Associates, San Rafael, California

ISBN 0-944197-62-0 (paperback)
ISBN 0-944197-63-9 (clothbound)

00 01 02 03 04   5   4   3   2   1

Contributing Photographers

TREE SWALLOW
Tachycineta bicolor

MORGAN BALL

FRANK S. BALTHIS

HERBERT CLARKE

RICK DAVITT

CLAIR DE BEAUVOIR

BRUCE FARNSWORTH

HOWARD T. FOLSOM

JEFF FOOTT

JOE FUHRMAN

NED HARRIS

JOHN HENDRICKSON

FRED HIRSCHMANN

GEORGE H. H. HUEY

RUSS KERR

RON LEVALLEY

ARTHUR MORRIS

B. MOOSE PETERSON

CHUCK PLACE

JEFFREY RICH

DENNIS SHERIDAN

BRIAN E. SMALL

HUGH P. SMITH, JR.

JACK TASOFF

CONNIE TOOPS

TOM VEZO

GEORGE WUERTHNER

BIRDER AT VERNAL POOL
Santa Rosa Plateau Preserve, managed by the Nature Conservancy, Riverside County

Birding offers opportunities to slow down and become acquainted
with the landscape from a fresh perspective.

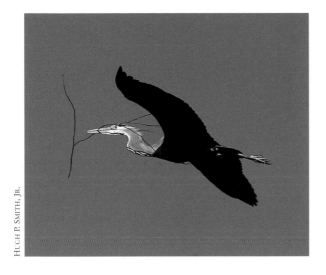

HUGH P. SMITH, JR.

California's Wild Birds

One spring day I hiked up to a local viewpoint to watch migrating birds. Unfurling oak leaves filled the air with promises of warblers and coming spring, the air smelled sweet, and for the first time in months the granite boulders exuded a soft warmth on their sunward sides. Lichen coated the rocks except where I had worn down a spot from previous watches. I had been coming here for weeks, scanning the sky in a census of the spring's first birds, and each day brought different birds, or none at all. I would find it hard to explain this passion; but the anticipation of seeing birds drew me back time after time—because you never know what bird you might see next when birding in California.

From the explosion of half a million Snow Geese erupting off a marsh, to coastal bays teeming with seabirds, to the brilliant flash of a Vermilion Flycatcher on a desert slope, there is nothing subtle about the wild birds of California. And with over six hundred species—roughly two-thirds of North America's birds—California lures both birds and the people who enjoy watching them.

This book offers tribute to California's tremendous wealth of wild birds and to the natural areas that sustain this abundance. Natural areas in California include nine national parks, thirty-seven national wildlife refuges, eighteen national forests and many more state and local preserves, parks, and wildlife areas. These wildland sanctuaries protect critical habitats and exuberant concentrations of birds.

GREAT BLUE HERON
Ardea herodias
Morro Bay
San Luis Obispo County

A crooked stick is just the thing for a comfortable nest—if you are a heron. During nest building, males present sticks to their mates, who either add the sticks to the nest or toss them away.

Such is the case with the Klamath Basin National Wildlife Refuges. Located on the California-Oregon border northeast of Mount Shasta, the Klamath Basin—a series of lakes, marshes and wetlands—has long served as one of the most significant refueling stops for migrating ducks and geese in the western states. Despite their enormous value to birds, the basin's lush marshes were being drained for agricultural purposes by the time Theodore Roosevelt set aside 81,619 acres as the Klamath Lake Reservation in 1908. Today, after nearly a century of restoration and land acquisition, six refuges in the Klamath Basin total more than 180,000 acres. Once more, it is possible to observe several million waterfowl, along with up to five hundred Bald Eagles, on a single frosty November morning. When these immense flocks take flight, the wild clamor of their cries and wingbeats will leave you breathless and linger forever in your memory.

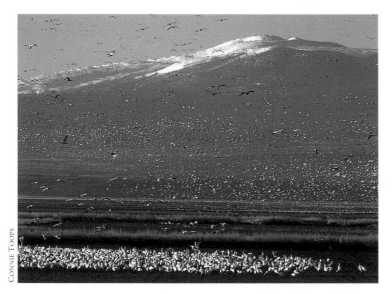

ROSS'S GEESE
Chen rossii
SNOW GEESE
Chen caerulescens
Tule Lake National Wildlife Refuge
Siskiyou County

Huge, late-winter flocks of geese congregating in the Klamath Basin fill the cold air with the thunder of their wings.

Even more special to me is another kind of landscape: the quiet overlooked parcels of land managed by the U. S. Forest Service, the Bureau of Land Management, and other agencies. Here, the hordes of birds and birders (as people who watch birds call themselves) are largely absent and it is easier to focus on the unique lives of individual birds. These pockets of land protect more than just single frenzied nodes of concentrated birds—they preserve the subtle, intact web of interrelationships that ties the landscape together, bird by bird, across vast distances. Here, in these sometimes small and scattered remains of wild lands, we find the true beating heart of healthy ecosystems.

My favorite birding site, near my home on the western slope of the Sierra Nevada, is one of these special pockets: a small, local hilltop managed by the Bureau of Land Management. This region of "monotonous" coniferous forest is largely ignored by birders and ornithologists—but is nevertheless the epicenter of my avian universe. From my worn boulder I can stand and monitor a slice of sky that stretches from the Sierra crest to the Coast Ranges. During the migration season, deadlines and desk duties fall by the wayside as I hike up to my lookout and stare into the sky for hours and days at a stretch. And for what? At best only a dozen hawks may pass by, or a couple groups of migrating cranes, or a few unidentified birds in the distance. Much of the time passes without a single feather stirring past, but this immersion in long empty spaces tunes my senses to nature's unpredictable drama. Then, just as I start thinking about leaving my little outpost, a trio of Yellow-rumped Warblers shoots past, chipping softly a thousand feet over the sparkling river canyon. With them my spirit soars to the horizon and imagining what else might show up I decide to stay a little longer.

Birds have always figured significantly in the human imagination. From the Neolithic bird-bone flutes discovered in China to the stunning flicker-feather headdresses worn by indigenous Californians during ceremonial dances, we see that birds embody a rich component of the human experience. Their freedom of flight has captivated us but so has the guileless exuberance of their lives, as when the exaggerated leaps and bows of courting cranes inspired ancient human dances. If you watch courting cranes yourself—like those that gather at the Cosumnes River Preserve south of Sacramento in late winter—you may find your heart, your mind, and perhaps your feet moving in contagious reflection.

Certainly, human efforts at flight—from balloons to jets—reveal another way that birds have inspired us. But even more evocative is the suggestion that birds gave us freedom through another form of expression: the written word. According to Greek mythology, the god Hermes designed the Greek alphabet—the cornerstone of western thought—after watching the patterns of cranes in flight. Perhaps the Greeks felt that language and flight were parallel expressions of freedom, as if either wings or words could capture flights of fancy.

HOWARD T. FOLSOM

GREAT EGRET
Ardea alba
Bolsa Chica Ecological Preserve
Orange County

Interactions between birds can be energetic and graceful, sometimes resembling complicated dances.

BIRDS IN FLIGHT

What exactly are these small, feathered beings with fiercely beating hearts that we call birds? In a sense, birds are simply warm-blooded reptiles covered in lacy scales we call feathers (only on their legs do birds still show true scales). One hundred and sixty million years ago an ancestral, reptile-like animal developed crude feathers that at first offered just a bit of warmth. Only later did these protofeathers evolve into a feature for flying. From

CALIFORNIA CONDOR
Gymnogyps californianus
Santa Barbara County
February, 1999

By 1985, the California Condor population had dropped so low that only one breeding pair survived in the wild. A highly controversial decision was made to bring all wild condors into a captive-breeding program. So far, over fifty condors have been returned to the wild as the captive population has grown. Number 8, shown here, was captive-born and raised, then released at the age of one year in late August, 1995. Now six years old, she is a dominant female and beginning to display courtship behavior with male condors in her area.

their humble beginnings, feathers have transformed into the most highly evolved epidermal structures known and now come in a mind-boggling variety of shapes and colors. One type of feathers, such as those that form the brilliant red gorget of some male hummingbirds, have no color of their own but serve merely as specialized mirrors that reflect certain wavelengths of light. Another type are the feathers of owls, designed less for color than for providing silent flight with a unique velvet texture that dampens the rustle of air against their wings.

Like feathers, the wings of birds take a wide variety of forms, each highly adapted to a specific mode of life. The long streamlined wings of a Peregrine Falcon facilitate that bird's extremely fast flight, while the short, broad wings of a Red-tailed Hawk are designed for sustained soaring. Despite these and many other variations, wings still show a remarkable degree of uniformity due to the aerodynamic constraints of flight. For instance, all wings in cross section have a streamlined, teardrop shape that slips effortlessly through the air and a slight camber that creates lift with a minimum amount of friction.

Flight also requires delicate balances between features that increase power and those that decrease weight. The breast muscles on a chicken are an example of the massive musculature that has evolved to power a bird's wings. On an albatross, feathers and breast muscles together account for forty-seven percent of the bird's weight. Yet flight also demands that a bird be light, so anatomical reductions offset the heavy feathers and wing muscles. Over millions of years, birds have slowly shed bone mass, given up heavy jaws and teeth, and eliminated skin glands. Birds have adapted to requirements of flight in many other ways, including compressing their breeding season into a narrow window of time so their reproductive organs can shrink for most of the year.

The effort of becoming airborne and staying aloft for significant amounts of time requires substantial power. Birds generate and sustain this power through a four-chambered heart with rapid circulation and a highly efficient respiratory system that includes a pair of lungs plus five pairs of air sacs. Furthermore, birds must consume exclusively energy-rich foods and have very swift and effective digestive systems. In essence, birds are supercharged metabolic "engines" that can digest roughly ninety-five percent of a meal's energy in as little as fifteen minutes. Their roaring metabolic fires burn close to the threshold of 116 degrees Fahrenheit where proteins begin to denature, but such are the apparent demands of flight.

Because of their need for energy-rich items, much of a bird's day may be spent searching for food. In frigid winter conditions, Black-capped Chickadees need to eat every few seconds just to maintain their high body temperature. In summer, hummingbirds will fill up on nectar every fifteen minutes if possible. To facilitate this search, each species of bird typically associates with a specific preferred habitat where it seeks food, water, and safe cover. Such species-habitat associations are fluid, fulfilling different birds' needs on a seasonal or even hourly basis. At the San Francisco Bay National Wildlife Refuge, shorebirds and gulls may rest and preen on elevated levees and berms one minute, then flock to nearby mudflats as soon as changing tides expose fresh food. Likewise, the Sacramento National Wildlife Refuge provides critical waterfowl resting habitat in winter but is used comparatively little during summer months when most waterfowl head north.

Clark's Nutcrackers illustrate how rich these relationships between organism and place can become. In the 1970s, observers discovered that these birds of high mountain forests have developed symbiotic relationships with several species of pines and subsist largely on a diet of pine seeds. During the abbreviated, late-summer harvest season, nutcrackers store enough seeds to survive on for the rest of the year. In two weeks a small, social flock of nutcrackers will collect and bury over four million seeds—about three times more than they need for their survival. Each nutcracker buries its own supply of food, pushing with its bill small groups of seeds into several inches of soil in locations that the bird memorizes. Even though a nutcracker may hide thirty thousand caches of seeds, they are still able to find them! Because more seeds are buried than are needed, many seeds survive to sprout into new generations of trees.

Scientists hypothesize that many subalpine pine forests within the nutcrackers' range might not exist without such careful plantings. The symbiotic relationship is further cemented by the evolution of special features on the pines that favor nutcrackers, such as cones positioned for maximum visibility to birds flying overhead and woody scales that hold the seeds in place until strong-billed nutcrackers come along to break them free. Nutcrackers have essentially "domesticated" pines by cultivating favorable genetic traits from a less nutritious wild form (you could also say that pines may have domesticated the nutcrackers!).

CLARK'S NUTCRACKER
Nucifraga columbiana
Eagle Lake, Lassen County

Noisy, curious nutcrackers are a familiar sight to anyone who has spent time in the mountains. The long, stout bills of these birds enable them to pry apart the thick scales of pine cones and extract the highly-nutritious seeds.

Extend the possibilities of this recently discovered symbiosis outward and you quickly realize that California landscapes host many fascinating—and perhaps, many still undiscov-

EURASIAN DOTTEREL
Charadrius morinellus
Lake Talawa, Del Norte County
September 9, 1992

The normal migration route of this Siberian bird takes it to north Africa, but on a few occasions strays have reached the coast of California. Most rare migrants, such as this individual, are juveniles unfamiliar with migration routes.

ered—relationships between birds and their environments. Until the 1980s, for instance, the highly secretive Black Rail was considered a very rare bird specific to coastal estuaries in the San Francisco Bay region (with another small population on the lower Colorado River); then two sharp-eared birders detected calling birds in a Sierra Nevada freshwater marsh. The discovery that Black Rails verge on common in an unexpected inland location completely changed presumptions about the habitat relationships of this little-known species and points to discoveries that have yet to be made.

Relationships between birds and their environments take on larger, global dimensions when we consider migratory birds. Over 450 of the 600-plus bird species that have been observed in California fall into this category and connect the state to other regions and other global climate processes (such as weather systems in the Southern Hemisphere). Pelagic birds—birds of the open ocean—venture from Arctic and Antarctic regions into California waters, thus demonstrating that California plays a vital role in the lives of sea-going birds who breed thousands of miles away.

Migrants to California from far-off regions can number in the millions, as with Sooty Shearwaters from New Zealand, or they may be exceedingly rare, as with Asiatic vagrants such as Eurasian Dotterels and Brown Shrikes. Another group of wanderers reaching California are songbirds of the eastern United States that get off track during migration and mistakenly head west until they hit the Pacific Ocean. Nearly all of the migratory eastern songbirds have been seen at one time or another at coastal birding hotspots like Point Reyes just north of San Francisco.

In addition to providing an extraordinary crossroads where many global patterns of bird movement converge, California hosts one of the most diverse landscapes in the world. The *Sunset Western Garden Book* notes that twenty-one of the twenty-four different climatic zones of the western United States occur within California, whereas most other states have only a few zones. Los Angeles County alone contains more major habitat types than any state but California and more than most countries in the world.

An imaginary journey around California serves to highlight some of this habitat diversity. Traveling west from the Sierra Nevada one crosses the broad Central Valley, with its remnant grasslands and waterlogged basins, then enters into the band of coastal ranges that stretch the length of the state. Beyond lie saltwater bays, estuaries, beaches, and headlands. Offshore an immensely productive cold water upwelling creates abundant food resources for seabirds. North along the coast one enters into rain-saturated forests from the Pacific Northwest, while southward one progresses into desert plains that continue across the Mexican border. Deserts curl around the southern portion of the state and bend northward along the eastern base of the Sierra Nevada, becoming increasingly colder and wetter as one travels north to the Oregon border. Within this mosaic live some five thousand native plant species, a thousand native vertebrates, and as many as three hundred biotic communities.

The towering Sierra Nevada accounts for some of California's greatest habitat diversity. Offering nearly 14,000 feet of elevational gradient across which biotic communities divide themselves, this mighty mountain range also raises a lofty wall that alters major weather systems. In fact, when the Sierra Nevada reached its current height two million years ago, it turned western California into a land of climatic sanctuary by shielding the state from frigid continental winters. Its elevated slopes also wring moisture out of maritime storms, providing the west slope with abundant supplies of water and turning the eastern side into desert.

Geographic and climatic factors associated with the Sierra Nevada uplift increase the number of niches available for additional species. This increase in diversity becomes evident if one examines clusters of ecologically-similar bird species while traveling upslope. Blue Grosbeaks of the Central Valley, for instance, are replaced by Black-headed Grosbeaks as one ascends into the foothill pine-oak belt; then Evening Grosbeaks take over in mountain forests only to give way to Pine Grosbeaks at high elevations. Similar transitions can be

B. MOOSE PETERSON/WRP

BRIAN E. SMALL

Left: CASSIN'S FINCHES
Carpodacus cassinii
Mammoth Lakes, Mono County

Above: PINE GROSBEAK
Pinicola enucleator
Yosemite National Park

Even though they have been given different names, these two species of seed-eating finches are very closely related and share a similar ecological niche. A diet of seeds enables them to survive year-round in the mountains.

PINE SISKINS
Carduelis pinus
Mammoth Lakes
Mono County

Some seed-eating birds, such as these Pine Siskins, remain in the mountains during the colder months. Fluffed feathers conserve warmth during a winter snowstorm.

traced between House Finches, Purple Finches, Cassin's Finches, and Gray-crowned Rosy-Finches—or between Gambel's Quail, California Quail, and Mountain Quail. Such distributions of species demonstrate that habitat diversity translates into species diversity. If a mountain slope were somehow transformed into one uniform habitat, only one species out of each cluster would probably end up surviving there.

SEASONS OF THE BIRD YEAR

Despite diversity in the places where they dwell, birds still follow a basic life history pattern, a standard cycle revolving around the four seasons. Thus, winter finds most birds retreating to secure areas. This retreat may simply involve a move downslope for species like Golden-crowned Kinglets and Red-breasted Nuthatches, while other species leave the state in search of warmer weather and more abundant food. Those species that wait out the coldest months in California usually do not waste energy defending territories but focus instead on finding their next meals. In the Central Valley, for instance, large gregarious flocks of blackbirds wander together in search of grain fields. Waterfowl congregate at secure marshy sites during the day and fly to surrounding fields to feed at night. The winter season is a time of minimal activity and birds spend time preening to maintain their warmth, feeding frequently, and sleeping in fluffed-out bundles.

Longer days trigger the behavioral condition known as *Zugunruhe*, an instinctive restlessness that nudges birds northward against the edges of the season. At the harsh frontier of spring lies a fine line that claims the lives of numerous birds each year, for early migrants that get first dibs on breeding territories may also be vulnerable to sudden setbacks in weather. Courageous Tree Swallows that push north into the face of storms may, with luck, arrive on their breeding grounds during a warm spell, or they may succumb to a late cold snap.

No one has definitively mapped the migratory pathways through California, but birders have collected observations from scattered sites that suggest possible routes. It appears that birds that have wintered in Mexico and further south funnel in a northwesterly direction across the Mexican deserts and pour into the lush corridor of vegetation and water along the Colorado River at the California-Arizona border. From here, they apparently cross low passes at the southern terminus of the Sierra Nevada and head northward up the Central Valley or through adjacent foothills. If it is still too cold to the north, then these migrants may bunch up in California's mild climate as they wait for a break in the weather.

At the same time that songbirds in Mexico are growing restless to strike north, huge numbers of waterfowl that have moved north from Mexico and California's Central Valley gather in the Klamath Basin of northern California. There they rest and add layers of fat before making long overland journeys as far north as the Arctic. Other species of waterfowl, along with a wide variety of migrating seabirds and shorebirds, prefer to travel along the coast. An observer watching from the seashore may witness a steady line of birds flying beyond the waves and not realize that many more birds are heading north even further offshore. This ocean route is little appreciated and seldom witnessed in its full splendor.

SNOW GEESE
Chen caerulescens
Klamath Basin Wildlife Refuges
Siskiyou County

When making long flights, waterfowl flocks fly in formations that reduce each bird's energy losses. While some ducks and geese travel great distances to breed in the Arctic, other species such as the Cinnamon Teal (page 98) nest in California.

In the state's mountain ranges, corresponding movements of songbirds are subtle, often taking place high overhead at night. By day, these birds trickle individually through oak groves and stands of pines. While ceaseless noise and activity fills the trees, you may not sense definite directional movement unless you follow the progress of a single bird. Sometime in April the collective energy of millions of birds heading north merges imperceptibly with the onset of breeding by local nesting birds. One day, migrating birds fill the trees with song; the next day, females sit on nests and males defend territories. It takes a fine level of attention for a human observer to track these changes, especially because some species continue migrating as others begin nesting.

It is a pleasure each spring to keep notes on the dates when species first appear, as I do from my local lookout. Over the course of years, these arrival dates shift like tides, reflecting the ebb and flow of climate. A mild winter translates into early arrivals; a delayed spring means late arrivals. In my neighborhood, it seems that warblers cue in on the first flush of oak leaves rather than weather, and I find myself watching the unfurling clusters of

TOWNSEND'S WARBLER
Dendroica townsendi
Joshua Tree National Park

Migration routes of many birds take them across desert regions far from their typical habitats. Songbirds, such as this Townsend's Warbler, may be found in great numbers as they search for food at patches of trees and water in the desert.

leaves as a signal to watch for newly-arrived species like Yellow-rumped Warblers. Oak moths lay their eggs on these tender young leaves, and migrating warblers arrive just in time to feast upon the emerging caterpillars.

After the frenzy of migration and the nesting season, bird activity becomes relatively subdued through the summer. Central Valley marshes lose their bright morning choruses of Marsh Wrens and Common Yellowthroats, while ducks molt into drab eclipse plumage and slip away into secluded areas. Waves beat against empty shorelines and hawks hunker down on shady perches. Dry, hot hillsides and grasslands become quiet and empty. Only high mountain peaks still buzz with birds taking advantage of the short, intense growing season. Patches of willows in mountain meadows may fairly burst with groups of songbirds. Warbling Vireos, Orange-crowned Warblers, Wilson's Warblers, Lincoln's Sparrows, and many other species may abound in alpine summer settings. Some of these colorful species have already raised their young at lower elevations—and then ascended the slopes to avoid the heat and find fresh food.

Fall migration is languid and dispersed in comparison to the urgency that characterizes spring migration. In the warm, ripe days of late summer it seems that few birds commence the long journey until absolutely necessary. If weather permits, many birds linger far north of their usual wintering grounds. Grebes, ducks, and other marshbirds often remain until freezing waters push them further south.

One of California's premier fall migration events occurs at Marin Headlands, where the largest concentration of migrating raptors in western North America gathers. Each fall, teams of volunteers organized by the Golden Gate Raptor Observatory have counted as many as thirty-six thousand hawks, eagles, and falcons. Nothing is more exhilarating to a birder than to stand on Hawk Hill in the Golden Gate National Recreation Area as Sharp-shinned Hawks, Cooper's Hawks, and occasional Peregrine Falcons streak past faster than you can count them. Then, as you turn and look down across San Francisco and the Bay, you may see a steady stream of hawks riding thermals over the ramparts of the Golden Gate Bridge.

For sheer numbers, however, few birding events top the annual fall gathering of Eared Grebes on the mirrored waters of Mono Lake, just east of Yosemite National Park. Roughly one million Eared Grebes from as far north as British Columbia gather at this inland sea to feed on superabundant brine shrimp and to fatten up for the next stage of their migration south. At sunrise, as the sun crests the Great Basin desert, the lake sparkles like a sea of jewels as birds dip their bills to feed and bathe. This spectacular gathering at Mono Lake offers one of few scenes that preserve the sense of North America's original wildlife abundance, yet it remains today only because of the work of a dedicated group of ornithologists, birders, and activists. Thanks to the efforts of the Mono Lake Committee and hundreds of other hard workers, Los Angeles' thirst for the lake's water has been regulated to protect the lake's long-term ecological health, giving grebes and other birds a place to rest.

FRANK S. BALTHIS

WATCHING BIRDS

Spectacular gatherings of birds also act as magnets for people. Whenever I set my spotting scope up in a public place, casual passersby will congregate and ask what I am looking at. Many will peek through the scope and exclaim "they had no idea." Once in a while, someone stops, completely transfixed by the sight of thousands of grebes or the stunning beauty of a single hawk. This instant of insight into the wonders of the natural world may be the very moment when a person becomes a budding birder.

My own transformation came when I was fifteen years old and single-mindedly hooked on chasing snakes, frogs, and salamanders. I had talked my way into an Audubon Society tour to Arizona simply because that was a great area for snakes and lizards. Little did I know I would spend fourteen days trapped in a van with a crew of crazy birders. Their assorted antics included stopping suddenly on freeway shoulders to run screaming in pursuit of fleeing birds. I was initially horrified by this strange bunch, but gradually fell into the spirit of the moment and came away a converted birder.

Watching birds is not only exciting, it is the fastest growing recreational activity in North America. Birding is, at the same time, one of the easiest outdoor activities and one of the most challenging—plus the equipment needs are minimal. Anyone with decent

CHRISTMAS BIRD COUNT CENSUS
Año Nuevo State Reserve
San Mateo County
December, 1985

Each year around Christmas, teams of birders count all the birds they can find within designated fifteen-mile circles. This tradition is over a century old and is the largest bird survey ever conducted. Currently, about 50,000 people participate each year in 180 count circles throughout the Western Hemisphere. Christmas Bird Counts are social, fun, and sometimes competitive; many birders consider this event the highlight of the year.

CHUCK PLACE/PLACE STOCK PHOTO

CALIFORNIA GULLS
Larus californicus
Mono Lake Tufa State Reserve
Mono County

Volunteers band gulls and record data as part of a twenty year gull study coordinated by Point Reyes Bird Observatory. Approximately 95 percent of the state's breeding population of California Gulls nest on islands at Mono Lake, making this inland sea an important site in the life cycle of this beautiful bird.

binoculars and a field guide may be as well equipped as the best expert. Even better, you merely have to step outside anywhere in California to begin. You can sit on a park bench, walk on the beach, take a boat out into the ocean, hike into a mountain wilderness, or just stand in your own yard and you will see birds. Starting with observations of a few birds that everyone knows—such as robins, crows, or pigeons—it is a simple task to expand your knowledge one new bird at a time. All kinds of books and classes will help speed up the process of learning birds, but spending time with local experts is the best and most enjoyable way to become proficient.

The astonishing bird life at California's refuges, parks, and preserves can be further explored in the company of naturalist-interpreters who know how to spot and describe birds and ecological processes. Many refuges offer interpretive visitor centers, trails, and brochures. Such sites have served as outdoor classrooms for generations of families and wildlife watchers.

While the majority of species are quite easy to identify regardless of a birder's skill level, birding becomes challenging as you push yourself to pick up finer points of identification. Some expert birders can differentiate bird species by the marks on single feathers or by the sound of single call notes in flight. Imagine being able to identify a hawk at four miles when it is merely a dot in your binoculars, looking only at how the dot moves. Imagine recognizing over eight hundred species of birds with only a momentary glance, and then being able to identify subspecies, age classes, sex, and feather wear on these birds! These are the unlimited challenges that can fill a lifetime with the fascination of watching birds.

These identification skills mean little, however, without an understanding of the landscapes and ecological niches that birds occupy. This environmental awareness is the other critical element of birding: learning how birds fit into and depend upon healthy landscapes. The folks who compassionately labored to save Mono Lake from the thirsty Los Angeles Department of Water and Power did so in part because they recognized that Eared Grebes and nesting California Gulls might have no other place to go if the lake was lost. With the loss of one lake—one key link in the life of a species—an entire population could

HERBERT CLARKE

HERBERT CLARKE

Left: MOUNTAIN CHICKADEE
Poecile gambeli
Angeles Crest
Los Angeles County

Above: BEWICK'S WREN
Thryomanes bewickii
Butterbredt Spring
Kern County

Birds that may be dismissed by many people as "little brown jobs," will reveal on closer scrutiny a great diversity of color, form, and behavior.

vanish. What starts as an interest in bird identification and learning to recognize sites that offer the best bird viewing may lead to advocating for the protection of such sites as they are threatened.

"Birding hotspots" is a term used to describe premier birding sites—places that attract many birds (as well as birders!). Hotspots are nearly always found at critical nodes in the landscape where food, water, or shelter for birds is concentrated. Hotspots include migration bottlenecks, such as shorelines where birds gather in preparation for crossing a large body of water or places where favorable wind currents concentrate migrating birds. Though it is merely a handful of cottonwoods around a cattle-trampled seep, Butterbredt Spring in the arid hills of eastern Kern County is a famous birding hotspot. A rare oasis on the difficult desert route between Mexico and western North America, the isolated spring proves very attractive to many species and great numbers of migrating songbirds.

Birders have an uncanny knack for finding points where birds and landscape converge, even when places like Butterbredt Spring require a long and difficult journey over bad roads. The search for new hotspots comprises one of the great joys and challenges of birding, and a visit to an already known hotspot is always cause for excitement. At their peak of activity, when all the conditions of wind, weather, and the timing of migration align, these sites may "drip" with birds—meaning that birds seem to ooze out of every pore of the landscape their numbers are so great. Dedicated birders live to witness these peak events.

The importance of hotspots goes beyond just good birding, however, for they some-times become conservation priorities among a broader community of scientists and land

WILLOW FLYCATCHER
Empidonax traillii
Santa Barbara County

Right: COASTAL CACTUS WREN
*Campylorhynchus brunneicapillus
sandiegense*
Palos Verdes Peninsula
Los Angeles County

*Bird species with declining or
imperiled populations require
constant monitoring. Researchers
compile detailed information on
the age, sex, and health of banded
birds. Banding—the technique
of placing numbered bands on a
bird's leg—is still the best way to
track individuals over their lifetime
with a minimum of disturbance.*

managers, as in the case of Mono Lake. In this way, birders have been likened to an "army" of eyes that fan out across the state each weekend, probing into new places, always alert for the unusual. The internationally acclaimed Cornell Laboratory of Ornithology in New York utilizes this network of eyes to collect scientific data through its innovative "Citizen Science" program. Even an activity as simple as recording birds identified at a backyard feeding station becomes a powerful conservation tool when results are pooled from hundreds of stations across the country. In this way, so-called "amateurs" have made many significant contributions to the field of bird study, and the history of ornithology in North America has been well-marked by cooperation between amateur birders and professional ornithologists.

Generations of records maintained by birders (many of which are now published in the journal *North American Birds)* have begun to highlight large-scale changes occurring over the face of North America. The observation that many species are expanding their range northward—as well as arriving much earlier on their nesting grounds—is notable in light of current concern about global warming. Unfortunately, such range expansions may mask the fact that overall population sizes of many birds are decreasing. However, there are exceptions for each of these observations: some species are expanding their range south-ward and some species are becoming much more numerous. Whatever conclusions may be drawn from the growing data, for the first time in history continuous records provide a window into the nature of bird populations and we are learning that populations and distribution ranges are not stable. In fact, both bird populations and their distributions are quite fluid, shifting amoeba-like in response to climate and landscape changes.

Observations of the flux occurring in bird populations puts birders at the cutting edge in monitoring poorly understood effects of global climate changes. In the spring of 1998—an El Niño year with warmer than average ocean temperatures—birders witnessed an unprecedented wave of Asian birds that poured into Alaska, over forty remarkable species and some in numbers ten times greater than previous counts. The same weather pattern brought Bristle-thighed Curlews to California's coast for the first time, along with one or two Gray-tailed Tattlers from Asia. In this way, birds prove to be an ideal barometer of perturbations in global climate: they are easily observed and counted; they readily fly to new regions in response to changing resources; and, legions of watchful birders quickly detect anomalies.

In addition to helping us monitor global climate changes, birds also signal more immediate and predictable disturbances to natural systems, such as those wrought by relentless habitat destruction. One of the most profound experiences of my life has been conducting annual bird surveys amongst several thousand acres of luxuriant oak woodlands slated for development. Each year I return to these stands as bulldozers gnaw incrementally into pristine stands of magnificent oaks. In front of the machines lie stupendous grasslands bursting with birdsong, and behind them sterile, freshly tarred streets and snarling lawn mowers. Nothing is more alarming than the resounding silence left as songbirds disappear, yet countless human neighborhoods over-look or accept this loss on a daily basis with not a word spoken to the local newspaper, city council, or state legislature.

With loss of habitat so go bird populations, and not far behind sinks the human spirit. Consider what our days would be like without the spontaneous exuberance of birdsong at sunrise. Consider how we lose the sense of wildness and beauty sparked by dazzling Lazuli Buntings and fluorescent Western Tanagers when the forests in which such birds live are lost. As our concrete grid grows, our encounters with wild birds become rarer, and it takes more effort to rediscover the birds in our lives. Yet many people make this effort every day, observing and listening to birds in backyards, neighborhood parks, and local wildlife refuges.

Generations of nature lovers have discovered their connection to the natural world

GEORGE WUERTHNER

GRAY-CROWNED ROSY-FINCH
Leucosticte tephrocotis
Mount Whitney
Sequoia National Park

On California's highest point, a hardy rosy-finch shares a hiker's simple snack. At these extreme elevations, this species finds a surprisingly bountiful feast in the supply of insects carried aloft by winds from the valleys below.

23

PHOTOGRAPHER AT SUNRISE
Bolsa Chica Ecological Reserve
Orange County

*A lone photographer shoulders
his equipment as dawn breaks
at a popular Southern California
birding site.*

through birds and there is probably no other group of wild organisms so widely observed and appreciated. Our lives are filled by memories of geese in autumn, by the rustle of finches in the brush, and by the rush of hummingbirds among flowers. Even from the cocoons of our automobiles we find connection to natural beauty in the quick flush of blackbirds from the roadside or in the silent vigil of hawks on fence posts. Birds accompany our walks, remind us that the sky is connected to the earth, and share with us our fields and gardens. There is value in honoring this close relationship between humans and birds as we roll their melodic names on our tongues, look deeply into the alert eyes of a sparrow, and sit quietly in their tangled homes of branches and shifting winds.

Birds hint at what it means to be human. They look back at us curiously as we watch them. Sometimes they sing in reply, or scold us if we whistle at them. But at the same time, birds are wild and independent of human intentions. They embody an ultimate freedom—the ability to travel unhindered across limitless space. Their wildness is part of our own wildness.

That spring day on my local lookout, I waited a long while after the Yellow-rumped Warblers had passed by, spellbound by the silence and the California hills that rolled off into the distance. Suddenly, a Sharp-shinned Hawk, intent on the northern horizon, flew out of the south. Small, delicate flyer, fierce hunter, bundle of tendons and reflexes that defied gravity, the Sharpie came in against the hillside below me and caught an updraft. Rising like a dry leaf on a whirlwind, she turned tight spirals against a thousand feet of sunlit canyon walls, then shot out on her northbound trajectory. For one moment, my breath caught as she glanced across her shoulder in passing. Thirty feet away, she locked my eyes in hers. And then she continued on her journey.

Heermann's Gull
Larus heermanni
La Jolla, San Diego County

After breeding on islands in the Gulf of California, Heermann's Gulls travel north to summer along the coasts of Oregon and Washington. In late summer they begin returning south where many winter on southern California beaches. Birders welcome the arrival of this strikingly colored gull each summer.

SNOW GEESE
Chen caerulescens
Tule Lake National Wildlife Refuge, Siskiyou County

Several million ducks and geese visit the Klamath Basin during their journey north, making it one of the most significant migration stopover points in the western United States.

Snow Geese *Chen caerulescens* · Ross's Geese *Chen rossii*
Tule Lake National Wildlife Refuge, Siskiyou County

The sudden sound of geese erupting into flight—rustling wings magnified thousands-fold along with
clamorous cries of countless birds—generates a thunderous, breathtaking roar.

NORTHERN HARRIER
Circus cyaneus
Tule Lake National Wildlife Refuge, Siskiyou County

Hawks and eagles wintering in the Klamath Basin may not bother to hunt and instead wait for ducks to die of natural causes. Here, a harrier stands guard over an American Wigeon.

TUNDRA SWANS *Cygnus columbianus* • BALD EAGLES *Haliaeetus leucocephalus*
Lower Klamath National Wildlife Refuge, Siskiyou County

*Winter birding in the Klamath Basin can be a very dramatic and memorable experience. Countless waterfowl
and hundreds of Bald Eagles congregate on frozen lakes, and the mountain views are spectacular.*

CANADA GEESE
Branta canadensis
Collins Lake, Yuba County

Powerful fliers, geese can reach speeds of fifty miles per hour. Only rarely do we see them closely enough to notice how they use their broad feet as rudders to help steer their flight.

CANADA GEESE
Branta canadensis
Woodleaf, Yuba County

Canada Geese chicks are precocial at birth, meaning they hatch covered with downy feathers, eyes open, and ready to swim. Aggressive pairs may take chicks from other parents and raise them as their own because large families gain higher status within the flock. These chicks will be able to fly in about two months.

JOHN HENDRICKSON

31

JOHN HENDRICKSON

SNOW GEESE
Chen caerulescens
Gray Lodge Waterfowl Management Area, Butte County

California's Central Valley is one of the world's great waterfowl wintering areas. In the past, flocks darkened the region's skies with clouds of countless birds. Refuges such as Gray Lodge keep this memory alive.

BREWER'S BLACKBIRDS
Euphagus cyanocephalus
Gray Lodge Waterfowl Management Area, Butte County

Blackbirds are highly gregarious birds, especially in winter. Here, a flock settles in for the night after a day scouring fields for seeds and grubs.

33

CLARK'S GREBES
Aechmophorus clarkii
Lower Klamath National Wildlife Refuge, Siskiyou County

Even though they are able to swim at birth, grebe chicks still prefer their parent's back for a safe and warm ride. When not peeking out, chicks snuggle down to sleep until the next meal.

MALLARD *Anas platyrhynchos* • AMERICAN COOTS *Fulica americana*
Lake Merritt Wildlife Refuge, Alameda County

A colorful male Mallard floats in a congregation of dark coots.

35

JEFFREY RICH

EARED GREBE
Podiceps nigricollis
Lower Klamath National Wildlife Refuge
Siskiyou County

*During summer, Eared Grebes build their
haphazard, floating nests on marshy lakes in
California's arid northeast corner. Their flimsy
nests may tilt precariously as the parents climb
aboard, and eggs may sit partly submerged in
cold water—but remarkably they still hatch.*

RED-TAILED HAWK
Buteo jamaicensis
Eagle Lake
Lassen County

Buteos—the soaring specialists among hawks— favor open country where they can ride powerful thermals for hours. From lofty viewpoints, they detect prey at three times the distances humans could see the same objects. This Red-tailed Hawk has an ideal home in a remote part of California.

CALIFORNIA GULLS
Larus californicus
Mono Lake Tufa State Reserve
Mono County

Floating effortlessly like kites on the wind, California Gulls keep watch over their nesting colony. With lake levels rising again, Mono Lake's gull colonies are now safe from four-legged predators that had been crossing exposed mudflats to eat eggs and chicks.

OSPREY
Pandion haliaetus
Eagle Lake, Lassen County

Osprey build huge, conspicuous nests near lakes and rivers. Because it takes so much energy to build structures of this size, the nests are used repeatedly, perhaps by generations of Ospreys. The smaller male Osprey brings fish to the nest where the female feeds herself and their chicks.

YELLOW-HEADED BLACKBIRDS
Xanthocephalus xanthocephalus
Mono Lake, Mono County

In an awkwardly vertical world, this pair somehow manages to nest and raise a family. As the female constructs a nest with wet aquatic weeds that dry and tighten into a secure structure woven between sturdy stems, the male perches above and sings his harsh, raspy "song."

NORTHERN FLICKER
Colaptes auratus
Lee Vining Canyon
Mono County

Like other primary cavity nesters, Northern Flickers favor aspens for nest sites. Once they cut a hole in the protective bark, they find the inner wood soft and easy to excavate.

BRIAN E. SMALL

Pygmy Nuthatch
Sitta pygmaea
Lee Vining Canyon
Mono County

*This diminutive bird is seldom encountered
outside of Ponderosa Pine forests. Except when
breeding, they gather in small, noisy flocks to
roam in search of conifer seeds.*

42

LEAST BELL'S VIREO
Vireo bellii pusillus
Santa Ynez Valley, Santa Barbara County

*Once abundant in riparian habitats from the Mexican border
to Red Bluff, this tiny songbird's population crashed to a low of 300 pairs in
the 1980s, when it was added to state and federal endangered species lists.
After intense efforts by various agencies and individuals, Least Bell's Vireo populations
in California have climbed back to 2,000 nesting pairs. Flood-control projects, grazing,
and Brown-headed Cowbird parasitism continue to be threats.*

MORGAN BALL

AMERICAN KESTREL
Falco sparverius
Refugio Canyon
Santa Barbara County

This beautiful falcon—barely larger than a robin—is well adapted to civilization, thriving around houses and farms if enough wild spaces are left in which it can hunt. Unlike most raptors, kestrels feed primarily on large insects.

GREAT HORNED OWL
Bubo virginianus
Sierra Foothills, Nevada County

*The widespread and highly versatile Great
Horned Owl ranges from Alaska to Argentina,
occupying virtually any habitat and often living
close to humans. Part of this success must be due
to this bird's overwhelming hunting ability, for
it eats anything it can capture, from skunks to
crawdads to hawks and other owls.*

FRED HIRSCHMANN

STELLER'S JAY
Cyanocitta stelleri
Sequoia National Park

Raucous Steller's Jays are hard to miss except during the breeding season. Then they become uncharacteristically quiet and sneaky in order to avoid drawing attention to their own nests. They are one of the most familiar birds of mountain forests, where no campground or picnic area is without its share of these bright blue birds.

BRIAN E. SMALL

AMERICAN DIPPER
Cinclus mexicanus
Aspendell Creek, Inyo County

John Muir had a particular fondness for the remarkable "water ouzel" he met in the high Sierra. These energetic little birds live along clear streams where they "fly" underwater, up to twenty feet deep, to search for aquatic insects. They are also able to walk on the bottoms of rivers in currents stronger than a human could stand.

BRIAN E. SMALL

Mountain Bluebird
Sialia currucoides
Lee Vining Canyon
Mono County

Mountain Bluebirds are secondary cavity nesters—
they do not excavate their own cavities but move
into holes evacuated by primary cavity species like
Northern Flickers (page 41). This is a fine arrange-
ment so long as there are enough cavities to go around.
In areas where bluebird populations are low because
of limited cavities, people can put out nest boxes that
bluebirds will readily use.

PINYON JAY
Gymnorhinus cyanocephalus
Lava Beds National Monument, Siskiyou County

The scientific name of Pinyon Jays means "naked nose," referring to the lack of feathers around their nostrils. Such feathers would get gummed up when Pinyon Jays pry open resinous pine cones for seeds. Of the world's 113 crows and jays only three species show this unique adaptation.

JOHN HENDRICKSON

Barn Owl
Tyto alba
Yuba County

Characterized by striking, heart-shaped faces, Barn Owls are placed in their own family separate from the "true owls." Often living in close association with humans, Barn Owls are a welcome neighbor because they eat so many mice.

MERLIN

Falco columbarius
Clear Lake, Lake County

Though petite in size, Merlins are astonishingly powerful hunters. With only a few flicks of their wings, they readily overtake any fleeing bird and can even capture dragonflies in mid-air. Merlins visit California in winter then return north to nest in Canada and Alaska.

JOHN HENDRICKSON

51

CALIFORNIA SPOTTED OWL
Strix occidentalis occidentalis
Woodleaf Creek Preserve, Butte County

The California race of Spotted Owl has not yet received the media attention of its highly-publicized northern cousin, but extractive timber practices threatening this owl's populations may soon end its relative obscurity. Although this gentle bird has no fear of humans, encounters are already rare.

CALIFORNIA SPOTTED OWL
Strix occidentalis occidentalis
Plumas National Forest, Butte County

Despite three-foot wingspans, Spotted Owls can swoop in without making a sound. Their silent stealth enables them to catch unsuspecting voles, woodrats, and flying squirrels at night in the dense woods.

WESTERN WOOD-PEWEE
Contopus sordidulus
Lee Vining Canyon, Mono County

This female wood-pewee has built a well camouflaged nest out of spiderwebs and fine plant fibers. Her three eggs will hatch within two weeks. The word pewee is an imitation of the call of the Eastern Wood-Pewee.

SHARP-SHINNED HAWK
Accipiter striatus
Cherry Lake, Tuolumne County

Accipiters, such as this Sharp-shinned Hawk, are forest hunters. Their short wings and long tails give them quick, highly maneuverable bursts of flight to snatch small birds within dense vegetation. People walking in forests are sometimes startled by the whoosh of a "Sharpie" rocketing past.

JOHN HENDRICKSON

JOHN HENDRICKSON

BREWER'S BLACKBIRDS
Euphagus cyanocephalus
Yosemite National Park

*A flock of blackbirds pauses in front
of spectacular Bridal Veil Falls.*

56

YELLOW-BILLED MAGPIE
Pica nuttalli
Near Millville
Shasta County

The world's entire population of Yellow-billed Magpies is found in California, where they favor open areas in the northern Central Valley. Giving the photographer an inquisitive stare, this member of the Crow Family reveals a legendary intelligence that reputedly equals that of chimpanzees and gorillas.

57

SAGE GROUSE
Centrocercus urophasianus
Near Crowley Lake, Mono County

Sagebrush habitats in California have been dramatically altered in the last century, leading to significant declines in Sage Grouse populations. At only a handful of remote, ancestral leks do males still practice their elaborate courtship displays.

JOHN HENDRICKSON

GREAT HORNED OWLS
Bubo virginianus
Sierra Foothills, Yuba County

When it comes to nesting, all other birds flee before the Great Horned Owl. This large owl does not build its own nests but takes over those of other birds—perhaps after eating the rightful owner. Fortunately, Great Horned Owls nest early in the year and are usually finished by the time other birds start nesting.

RON LEVALLEY

GREAT GRAY OWL
Strix nebulosa
Prairie Creek Redwoods State Park, Humboldt County

The largest of North American owls—with a wingspan of five feet—the Great Gray is a phantom ghost of mountain coniferous forests. Just over a hundred of these regal owls reside in the state (with occasional winter visitors showing up some years) and few Californians have seen one here.

RON LEVALLEY

GREAT BLUE HERON
Ardea herodias
Arcata Marsh, Humboldt County

After two years of political battle, the city of Arcata won approval in 1979 to replace conventional chemical sewage treatments with a biological method using a series of freshwater marshes. These marshes, now a national model, provide habitat for over 200 species of birds while at the same time naturally filtering two million gallons of effluent a day.

RED-WINGED BLACKBIRD
Agelaius phoeniceus
Arcata Bottoms, Humboldt County

During the breeding season, male Red-winged Blackbirds prominently display their red shoulder patches.
These patches, also known as epaulets, provide a way to signal territorial intent. Males whose patches
have been experimentally covered quickly lose their territories.

Black Oystercatcher
Haematopus bachmani
Monterey Bay, Monterey County

The oystercatcher's unique bill is compressed from side to side, turning it into a stout chisel for plucking limpets from rocks and prying open tightly closed clams. These birds carve out a living in the turbulent zone where waves crash unpredictably against offshore rocks.

BROWN PELICAN
Pelecanus occidentalis
Santa Cruz, Santa Cruz County

Pelicans readily learn where to find easy meals. Once endangered, Brown Pelicans are now a common sight about wharves and harbors.

GREAT EGRET
Ardea alba
Elkhorn Slough, Monterey County

Egrets and Herons have their own characteristic flight silhouette—heads pulled in against the body and long legs trailing behind.

TUFTED PUFFIN
Fratercula cirrhata
Farallon Islands
West of San Francisco Bay

This puffin returns from a dive with fresh food for its chicks. The white face and comical ear tufts are breeding marks that disappear in winter birds.

COMMON MURRES
Uria aalge
Point Reyes National Seashore, Marin County

Once nearly extirpated by a lucrative fresh egg industry, murres made a rapid recovery in the late twentieth century. Coastal seabird colonies remain vulnerable, however, and many in California are closely monitored. Oil spills and changing ocean temperatures are current threats.

RON LeVALLEY

LONG-BILLED CURLEW
Numenius americanus
Mill Valley, Marin County

Largest of the North American shorebirds—and certainly the one with the longest bill—Long-billed Curlews are noisy residents of wet meadows. As these habitats are converted to agriculture and other developments, curlew populations have declined.

CALIFORNIA CLAPPER RAIL
Rallus longirostris obsoletus
Palo Alto Baylands, San Mateo County

Three races of endangered Clapper Rails occur in California. The race obsoletus *(shown here) once ranged from Humboldt Bay to Morro Bay, but survives today primarily in the south San Francisco Bay. These secretive, long-legged birds spend their entire lives within dense coastal salt marsh vegetation and they are highly vulnerable to disturbance and habitat fragmentation.*

CASPIAN TERN
Sterna caspia
San Francisco Bay, San Mateo County

Of all the terns, the Caspian Tern has the longest period of parental care. Nests are simple scrapes in the sands of beaches on undisturbed islands.

FRANK S. BALTHIS

BROWN PELICANS
Pelecanus occidentalis
Año Nuevo State Reserve, San Mateo County

By 1969, Brown Pelican populations had been hit so hard by use of the pesticide DDT that only five chicks were raised in California that year. These once endangered birds have slowly re-established themselves, yet their nesting colonies remain highly vulnerable to disturbance. The appearance of one person or dog may cause an entire colony to abandon its eggs and chicks.

TURKEY VULTURE
Cathartes aura
Antelope Valley, Kern County

The bend halfway out on a bird's wing is its wrist, meaning that the outer half of the wing corresponds to a hand. The inner half is the forearm and a bird's elbow is hidden in body feathers. Here, a vulture gets a jump start from the sun to start the day.

BALD EAGLE
Haliaeetus leucocephalus
Klamath Basin, Siskiyou County

The Bald Eagle—our national symbol—also represents the success of the Endangered Species Act as once endangered populations have rebounded under strict Federal protection. Birders visit the Klamath Basin National Wildlife Refuges to see the largest concentration of wintering Bald Eagles in the continental United States.

WESTERN GULLS
Larus occidentalis
Año Nuevo State Reserve, San Mateo County

Gulls play a valuable role as nature's cleaning crew. Here they gather to feast on placenta at an Elephant Seal birthing ground.

WESTERN GULL
Larus occidentalis
Anacapa Island, Channel Islands National Park

Islands along the California coast are critical sites for nesting Western Gulls.
Anacapa Island protects one of the largest colonies.

SANDHILL CRANE
Grus canadensis
Carrizo Plain, San Luis Obispo County

Standing nearly five feet tall, Sandhill Cranes are conspicuous winter visitors to open, wet meadows and grasslands of the Central Valley, where they feed on a variety of vertebrates and invertebrates, practice their exuberant courtship dances, and fill the air with their rolling, bugle-like calls. With spring's arrival, they migrate in long lines over the Sierra Nevada to breeding areas that stretch from northeastern California to the Arctic.

WESTERN MEADOWLARK
Sturnella neglecta
Maricopa, Kern County

This bird of open grasslands is well camouflaged unless it turns to reveal its brilliant front side. To attract a mate, this male sings loudly from high perches and shows off its colorful breast.

BAND-TAILED PIGEON
Columba fasciata
Santa Barbara Botanic Garden, Santa Barbara County

*Once hunted to the edge of extinction, this large and beautiful pigeon remains wary of humans
even though its populations have recovered. Throughout much of the year, Band-tailed Pigeons
wander in nomadic flocks searching for acorn and seed crops.*

TRICOLORED BLACKBIRD
Agelaius tricolor
Glenville, Kern County

Virtually the world's entire population of Tricolored Blackbirds lives and breeds in California with only a few small colonies crossing over the state's line. This species has experienced precipitous population declines due to urban expansion and intensified agricultural practices. Statewide surveys revealed a drop from 330,000 birds in 1994 to fewer than 95,000 in 1999.

CLAIR DE BEAUVOIR

ISLAND SCRUB-JAY
Aphelocoma insularis
Santa Cruz Island, Channel Islands National Park

First described as a distinct species in 1886, this large scrub-jay with intense blue feathers was later considered merely a geographic race unique to Santa Cruz Island. Species status was re-established in 1995. Today, visitors to the island will see one of California's "newest" birds.

SAN MIGUEL SONG SPARROW
Melospiza melodia micronyx
San Miguel Island, Channel Islands National Park

A classic Channel Islands scene: an endemic Song Sparrow perching on a distinctive Channel Islands plant, the Giant Coreopsis, Coreopsis gigantea. *This Song Sparrow, found only on San Miguel Island, is one of seventeen currently recognized endemic races of birds found on the Channel Islands.*

81

B. MOOSE PETERSON/WRP

KILLDEER
Charadrius vociferus
Morro Marsh, San Luis Obispo County

Killdeers are one of the most versatile birds. They like open spaces and readily use vacant lots, schoolyards, unpaved parking lots, and the many other areas cleared by humans. Their ringing kill-deer *calls are a familiar sound.*

SNOWY PLOVERS
Charadrius alexandrinus
Chick, left, San Luis Obispo County
Adult nesting, right,
McGrath State Beach, Ventura County

*This diminutive shorebird is one of the rarest in California,
requiring undisturbed ocean beaches for nesting. Vehicles, dogs,
beach-front development, and even strolling humans may all cause
this reclusive species to abandon its exposed nests. At only a handful
of locations do Snowy Plovers still dart about in pursuit of invertebrates
to feed their growing chicks, and intensive efforts are underway
to safeguard these sites.*

MORGAN BALL

RED-TAILED HAWKS
Buteo jamaicensis
San Marcos Foothills, Santa Barbara County

Resting on a nest platform that they nearly outgrow, these chicks will be ready to fly a month and a half after leaving the egg. The young hawk that hatches a day or two ahead of the other tends to be larger and have a better chance of survival if food is scarce.

MORGAN BALL

RED-TAILED HAWK
Buteo jamaicensis
San Marcos Foothills, Santa Barbara County

As creatures of sight, hawks have eyeballs that are equivalent in size to those of humans and disproportionately large for their small heads. So large are their eyes that their eye sockets meet in the center of their skull! Photographed from a blind, this Red-tailed Hawk feeds on a crow.

BLACK-CHINNED HUMMINGBIRD
Archilochus alexandri
Rocky Nook Park, Santa Barbara County

Carefully situated under an umbrella of leaves, this female hummingbird stands guard through rain or shine.
Her tiny nest—woven together with spider webs—will stretch to accommodate the rapidly growing chicks.

Nests, clockwise from upper left:
CALIFORNIA GNATCATCHER *Polioptila californica*
(parastized by a cowbird egg)
WESTERN GULL *Larus occidentalis*
RED-WINGED BLACKBIRD *Agelaius phoeniceus*
GREAT-TAILED GRACKLE *Quiscalus mexicanus*

Portraits, clockwise from upper left:
CLARK'S GREBE *Aechmophorus clarkii*
BROWN PELICAN *Pelecanus occidentalis*
LINCOLN'S SPARROW *Melospiza lincolnii*
BRANDT'S CORMORANT *Phalacrocorax penicillatus*

REDHEAD DUCK
Aythya americana
Mission Bay, San Diego County

*Redheads breed primarily in upper midwestern prairies and Great Basin marshes,
but a fair number winter in California, including southern coastal areas.*

JOE FUHRMAN

DOUBLE-CRESTED CORMORANT
Phalacrocorax auritus
Marina del Rey, Los Angeles County

With legs set far back on its body and all four toes joined by broad webbing, a cormorant is a superb swimmer and diver. This bird shows two white tufts of feathers on its head (a double crest) that are present only briefly in the breeding season.

AMERICAN COOT
Fulica americana
Del Rey Lagoon, Los Angeles County

Coots have remarkable feet that suggest a cross between long-toed rails and web-footed ducks. Youngsters do not look anything like their parents.

CALIFORNIA QUAIL
Callipepla californica
Point Mugu State Park, Los Angeles County

While a quail covey forages for seeds and insects, one of the birds will always stand lookout for predators. Males are brightly colored and possess a funny curled topknot.

BRIAN E. SMALL

WRENTIT
Chamaea fasciata
Santa Monica Mountains, Los Angeles County

Wrentits show no close affinity to any other songbird in North America, and taxonomists shuffled them from family to family before agreeing to place them in the Old World group called Babblers. Pairs mate for life and spend all their time together on a tiny two-acre territory that they never leave.

RED-BREASTED MERGANSER
Mergus serrator
Marina del Rey, Los Angeles County

Although included with the ducks, mergansers are distinct in having narrow, spear-like bills.
The name serrator *refers to backward-pointing serrations on the bill that help hold captured fish.*

MALLARD
Anas platyrhynchos
Upper Newport Bay Ecological Reserve
Orange County

With body and feathers fully extended to serve as a brake, this Mallard negotiates the delicate transition from air to water.

RUSS KERR

95

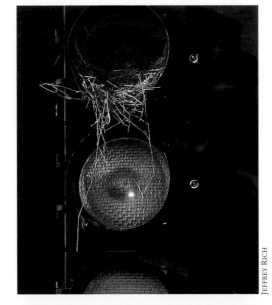

BURROWING OWL
NEST

DO NOT
FILL, BURY,
OR GAS

Clockwise from upper left:
HEERMANN'S GULL *Larus heermanni*
BREWER'S BLACKBIRD *Euphagus cyanocephalus*
FERRUGINOUS HAWK *Buteo regalis*
BURROWING OWL *Athene cunicularia*

ACORN WOODPECKER
Melanerpes formicivorus
Near Glenville, Kern County

If this species has any special requirements, it is an abundant supply of acorns and a place to store them. These hoarded acorns—up to 50,000 at a single site—serve as a "pantry" until the next harvest.

CINNAMON TEAL
Anas cyanoptera
Upper Newport Bay Ecological Reserve, Orange County

Flaunting his colorful patch of wing feathers is part of a Cinnamon Teal's courtship display. This patch, known as a speculum (the ancient Roman word for a mirror), is well represented on males of all dabbling ducks, with each species showing different colors.

HOWARD T. FOLSOM

RESIDENTS AND VISITORS AT NEWPORT BAY

On a rare, crystal-clear winter day with exceptional visibility of the San Bernardino Mountains, people enjoy walking, jogging, cycling, and birding at a neighborhood estuary. With careful planning, birds and bird habitats add great value to a community's quality of life.

WILLETS *Catoptrophorus semipalmatus* • MARBLED GODWITS *Limosa fedoa*
Upper Newport Bay Ecological Reserve, Orange County

While accurate counts are impossible, the number of shorebirds that use estuaries on the West Coast may be in the millions. Estuaries provide abundant food supplies unmatched by any other habitat, yet in the twentieth century 96% of the coastal estuaries between Morro Bay and Mexico were lost.

AMERICAN AVOCET
Recurvirostra americana
Tijuana River Mouth, San Diego County

It almost seems that Mom is instructing her attentive youngster on the proper way to sit avocet-style. Both parents help raise the chicks, with the male avocet being recognized by his longer and straighter bill.

BRIAN E. SMALL

101

CALIFORNIA GNATCATCHER
Polioptila californica
Coastal sage scrub near Irvine, Orange County

Caught in a moment of repose, the threatened California Gnatcatcher sits at the center of intense cross-fire as southern California developers eye what little remains of its coastal sage scrub habitat. An innovative Natural Communities Conservation Planning program, emphasizing voluntary cooperation between landowners and agencies, is attempting to develop regional plans that concentrate on habitat preservation.

BELDING'S SAVANNAH SPARROW
Passerculus sandwichensis beldingi
Bolsa Chica Ecological Reserve, Orange County

This nonmigratory Savannah Sparrow of southern California coastal salt marshes occupies a very narrow and fragmented habitat—mats of Pickleweed growing just above the high tide mark. Consequently, this sparrow's population hovers around 2,000 breeding pairs, a significant portion of which reside at Bolsa Chica Ecological Reserve.

WHITE-TAILED KITE
Elanus leucurus
Irvine, Orange County

White-tailed Kites have flourished and expanded their range in the last half century as agriculture converted diverse habitats to open fields, creating an exponential increase in the kite's favorite food—voles and small rodents.

OSPREY
Pandion haliaetus
Upper Newport Bay Ecological Reserve, Orange County

Genetic studies suggest that Ospreys are kites that have evolved to plunge-fish, a technique of diving completely into water to catch fish. Ospreys will often carry a fish as they migrate so they can snack on the wing.

RUSS KERR

BLACK SKIMMER
Rynchops niger
Bolsa Chica Ecological Reserve
Orange County

*"Skimming" for fish must be one of the most
unusual feeding methods in the bird kingdom.
When their long lower mandibles touch a fish,
skimmers instantly clamp down to catch it.
Because skimming wears down the lower
mandible, it grows twice as fast as the upper.*

BLACK-NECKED STILT
Himantopus mexicanus
Bolsa Chica Ecological Reserve, Orange County

If only stilts did have little front supports when they sat on the ground! But those are the legs of a chick that thinks it is well hidden.

RUSS KERR

GREAT EGRET
Ardea alba
Bolsa Chica Ecological Reserve, Orange County

Halfway out on wings a couple of small feathers extend from a bird's "thumb." These feathers are lifted to send a rush of air over the top of the wing, thus reducing turbulence and preventing stalling at slow speeds, as when this egret coasts to a landing.

ELEGANT TERNS
Sterna elegans
Bolsa Chica Ecological Reserve
Orange County

In 1959, this large tern of northwestern Mexico was first discovered nesting in the United States at San Diego. A breeding colony at Bolsa Chica started in 1986 and has since grown to well over a thousand pairs. This species now ranges as far north as San Francisco Bay.

RICK DAVITT

109

GREAT BLUE HERONS
Ardea herodias
Bolsa Chica Ecological Reserve, Orange County

In a courtship display that includes howling, clapping bills, shaking heads, and stroking each other with their bills,
a pair of Great Blue Herons finally gets down to the business of mating. At this point, the pair has already built
a nest together as a way of confirming each other's ability to be a dutiful partner.

RUSS KERR

BLACK-CROWNED NIGHT-HERON
Nycticorax nycticorax
Bolsa Chica Ecological Reserve, Orange County

To prevent from being attacked by "day" herons, night-herons often resort to feeding at night so they have the marshes to themselves. This must be a successful strategy because the Black-crowned Night-Heron is the most cosmopolitan and perhaps the most abundant heron in the world.

RED-SHOULDERED HAWK
Buteo lineatus
San Joachin Wildlife Sanctuary, Orange County

Extraordinary colors characterize California's Red-shouldered Hawks, which form a distinct population geographically isolated from Red-shouldered Hawks of the eastern United States. This beautiful bird will tolerate human neighbors so long as tall trees are left for it to nest in.

RUSS KERR

RUSS KERR

NORTHERN HARRIER
Circus cyaneus
Bolsa Chica Ecological Reserve
Orange County

This harrier uses all its feathers in making an agile about-face turn.

LOGGERHEAD SHRIKE
Lanius ludovicianus
San Joachin Wildlife Sanctuary
Orange County

Shrikes share the hooked bill and hunting style of raptors but lack strong feet. Thus they impale their prey to hold it while they tear off morsels.

BROWN PELICANS
Pelecanus occidentalis
La Jolla, San Diego County

The breeding plumage of Brown Pelicans includes a chestnut stripe down the neck and a bright red pouch that is displayed during a complex courtship ritual. The pouch also serves as a dip net for catching fish and is laced with blood vessels to help cool down these birds.

SURF SCOTER
Melanitta perspicillata
Bolsa Chica Ecological Reserve, Orange County

The Surf Scoter's scientific name perspicillata, *meaning spectacular, is an appropriate reference to the male's colorful face. Adapted to marine environments, these birds use their stout bills to crack open molluscs and crustaceans.*

GAMBEL'S QUAIL
Callipepla gambelii
Santa Rosa Mountains, San Bernardino County

Gambel's Quail inhabit arid desert regions avoided by the closely related California Quail (page 92).

116

JACK TASOFF

CALIFORNIA THRASHER
Toxostoma redivivum
Anza-Borrego Desert State Park, San Diego County

As the largest member of the Mockingbird Family, California Thrashers share the typical mockingbird trait of mimicking other bird songs. They also have strong legs and spend most of their lives on the ground digging in the soil and raking leaves with their extra-long bills.

WHITE-CROWNED SPARROW
Zonotrichia leucophrys
Anza-Borrego Desert State Park, San Diego County

This bird of mountains and northern regions spends its winters in the lowlands and southern deserts. In some parts of California, White-crowned Sparrows can be found year-round, but the birds that overwinter are a different subspecies than those that arrive in spring to breed.

JEFF FOOTT

VERDIN
Auriparus flaviceps
Joshua Tree National Park

Only four inches in length, the Verdin is one of North America's smallest birds. It has the added distinction of being unrelated to any other bird in the Western Hemisphere. These tiny desert dwellers supplement their insect diets by slitting open the bases of ocotillo flowers and stealing nectar.

BRIAN E. SMALL

WESTERN TANAGER
Piranga ludoviciana
Joshua Tree National Park

The large and flamboyant Tanager Family includes many of the most beautiful birds in the world. Over two hundred species live in the American tropics but only four wander north to breed in the United States. The Western Tanager is common in California's mountain forests.

PAINTED BUNTING
Passerina ciris
Joshua Tree National Park

The joy of birding at desert oases during spring migration lies in seeing something totally unexpected. Painted Buntings are exceedingly rare in California, though a couple show up each year. This colorful bird is far from its breeding grounds in Texas and Louisiana.

COSTA'S HUMMINGBIRD
Calypte costae
Joshua Tree National Park

Because hummingbirds' bodies consist of little more than a bundle of hard-working wing muscles and a big, fast-beating heart, these birds need a steady supply of food. To help meet this requirement, they have a complex spatial memory that enables them to track the location and productivity of each flower in their territory.

122

PHAINOPEPLA
Phainopepla nitens
Morongo Valley
Riverside County

*Phainopeplas belong to an odd group of four species
known collectively as the Silky Flycatcher Family.
Although these are birds of the American tropics,
the Phainopepla extends its breeding range into the
southwestern United States. Males are shiny black
and females gray, but both have the startling red eye.
Some individuals may first nest in desert regions, then
move either north or west to nest a second time in
cooler parts of the state.*

JOE FUHRMAN

SOUTHWESTERN WILLOW FLYCATCHER
Empidonax traillii extimus
Kern River, Kern County

*As part of a strategy to keep her nest hidden from predators, this female Willow Flycatcher carries away her chicks' fecal sacs
so they do not accumulate on the ground under the nest. An estimated 70 pairs of this race survive in California, many of
them at the Kern River Preserve which protects one of the state's most significant tracts of intact riparian habitat.*

INYO CALIFORNIA TOWHEE
Pipilo crissalis eremophilus
Ridgecrest, Inyo County

While the six subspecies of California Towhee are very similar in appearance, the Inyo race is distinct in being geographically isolated. Limited to a small area of rocky desert in the Argus Range west of Death Valley National Park, some 300 survive in tiny pockets of riparian vegetation.

JOE FUHRMAN

LESSER GOLDFINCH
Carduelis psaltria
Palm Desert, Riverside County

Though plainly adorned, the diminutive Lesser Goldfinch has a sweet scientific name. The Greek word psaltria *means "lute player," probably in reference to this bird's song.*

126

BULLOCK'S ORIOLE
Icterus bullockii
Joshua Tree National Park

Bullock's Orioles are familiar birds for their conspicuous colors—and for their nests, which hang from the branches of deciduous trees like socks made of fishing lines, hairs, and silvery plant fibers. Their ringing songs (both males and females sing) are as loud in volume as this male is bright in color.

Cactus Wren
Campylorhynchus brunneicapillus
Mojave Desert, San Bernardino County

*Living up to its name, the Cactus Wren spends much of its time surrounded by cacti. Here they find a place
for their large, bulky nests that is safe from snakes and other predators. When foraging, these wrens use their
long bills to lift small objects and uncover seeds and small insects.*

GREATER ROADRUNNER
Geococcyx californianus
Palm Desert, Riverside County

Blessed with strong legs and leg muscles plus a long, rudder-like tail for balance and maneuverability, roadrunners overpower most prey in fifteen-mile-per-hour sprints. Its common name stems from an old habit—running along roads in front of horse-drawn carriages.

CLAIR DE BEAUVOIR

BURROWING OWLS
Athene cunicularia
Imperial Valley
Imperial County

*These long-legged, ground-loving owls nest in old mammal burrows.
Burrowing Owls use two strategies to conceal their vulnerable chicks
from predators: they line their burrows with chips of manure to disguise
the smell that would attract snakes, and they utter a rattlesnake-like
chatter to frighten mammalian predators. Yet against agricultural
development and urban sprawl they are defenseless and their
populations have suffered mightily.*

GILA WOODPECKER
Melanerpes uropygialis
Winterhaven, Imperial County

Once common in Imperial County, this striking species has been reduced to a few pairs. Continued destruction of native riparian habitat along the lower Colorado River further places this species at risk. Their traditional nesting sites include cavities they excavate in saguaro cacti—a messy job since cactus juices stick to their feathers. They wait a year for that cactus cavity to dry out and harden before building a nest.

WHITE-WINGED DOVE
Zenaida asiatica
Imperial Valley, Imperial County

In the harsh desert environments where they nest, these doves often fly up to twenty-five miles for food and water. Cactus fruits may at times provide their only water source. The genus name Zenaida *is a tribute to Princess Zénaide Charlotte Julie Bonaparte, the wife of a famed French naturalist.*

YELLOW-HEADED BLACKBIRD
Xanthocephalus xanthocephalus
Salton Sea
Imperial County

Beautiful native bird meets widely-cursed invasive plant. The wildfire-like spread of tamarisk has severely impacted the ecological health of riparian habitats in the Southwest.

133

WOOD STORKS
Mycteria americana
Salton Sea, Imperial County

A small and steadily diminishing group of these endangered birds visit the south end of the Salton Sea each summer. Most of these visitors are immatures, not yet ready to breed.

DOUBLE-CRESTED CORMORANT
Phalacrocorax auritus
Salton Sea, Imperial County

If one image could capture the fragile balance facing California's wild birds, this would be it—birds surrounded by a polluted manmade sea that offers both risk and refuge. Here, as elsewhere in California, hard-working volunteers and organizations struggle to preserve the ecological integrity of bird habitats and the quality of life we share with these wondrous creatures.

135

CLAIR DE BEAUVOIR

BLUE GROSBEAK
Guiraca caerulea

Acknowledgements

Many thanks to Jane Freeburg and Mark Schlenz of Companion Press for nurturing the idea of this book over years of discussions and then bringing it to fruition with such care and skill. This has been a fun collaborative project. I am immensely grateful to Ted Beedy, Tavia Cathcart, Allen Fish, Nelson Foster, and Liese Greensfelder for careful readings and insightful comments on early drafts of the essay. Finally, I thank the photographers whose remarkable images convey so well the character of California's colorful birds.